CRYPTO TRADING FOR BEGINNERS

A beginner's guide to trading and investment strategies in cryptocurrency

Abraham Robert. C

Copyright©2024 Abraham Robert .C

All Rights Reserved

TABLE OF CONTENT

CHAPTER ONE _____ 11

An overview of cryptocurrencies _____ 11

Operations of cryptocurrency _____ 12

Numerous Advantages of Cryptocurrency _____ 14

Some examples of cryptocurrencies _____ 15

    Bitcoin _____ 15

    Ethereum _____ 16

    Litecoin _____ 16

    Ripples _____ 17

CHAPTER TWO _____ 19

Cryptocurrency scams and security _____ 19

Fraudulent websites _____ 19

Online Ponzi schemes _____ 19

Endorsements from famous people _____ 20

Romance scams _____ 21

Is it safe to use cryptocurrency _____ 22

Cryptocurrency security _____ 24

Cryptography _____ 24

    Transaction Security _____ 26

    Cryptography based on public keys _____ 27

    Hash Functions _____ 28

    Encryption _____ 29

    Digital Signatures _____ 30

CHAPTER THREE _____ 33

A Guide to Block-chain Technology _____ 33

How Does Block-chain Work _____ 33

Significance of block-chain technology _____ 35

The operations of block-chain technology _____ 36

Block-chain Decentralization _____ 39

Benefits of Block-chain _____ 41

    A Higher Level of Safety _____ 41

    Enhancement of Accuracy _____ 42

    Increased Productivity and Efficiency _____ 43

Block-chain related challenges _____ 43

    Restrictions on Transactions _____ 44

    The Consumption of Energy_____ 44

    Problems with Scalability _____ 45

    Concerns Regarding Regulation _____ 46

Applications and Use Cases of Block-chain Technology _____ 47

    Banks and lenders _____ 47

    Smart Contracts _____ 48

    Cyber security_____ 49

    Medical care _____ 50

    The logistics _____ 51

    NFTs _____ 51

Different types of block-chain _____ 52

    Public block-chain_____ 52

    Private block-chain _____ 53

    Consortium Block-chain _____ 54

    Hybrid Block-chain _____ 55

A Brief History of Block-chain _____ 55

CHAPTER FOUR _____ 59

Cryptocurrency investment opportunities _____ 59

Investing in Cryptocurrency: Some Safeguards to Consider _____ 59

    Education and Research _____ 59

- Components of Block-chain _____ 59
- Having an Understanding of Cryptocurrency _____ 60
- Analysis of the Market _____ 60
- Assessment of the Risk _____ 61
- Useful Resources for Education _____ 61

    Make sure to use reliable exchanges _____ 62

- Security Features _____ 62
- Complying with the Regulations _____ 62
- Trading Volume and Liquidity _____ 62
- User Experience _____ 63
- Reputation in the Community _____ 63

    Diversify the investments you have _____ 64

- Distribution of Assets _____ 64
- The Management of Risk _____ 64
- The Rebalancing of Portfolios _____ 65
- Long-Term Perspective _____ 65

    Use hardware wallets for long-term storage _____ 66

- Cold Storage Solutions _____ 66
- Procedures for Backing Up _____ 66
- Perform Routine Maintenance _____ 67

    Enable two-factor authentication (2FA) _____ 67

- Stronger Safety Measures 67
- Techniques for Authentication 68
- Codes for backups 68
- Checks and Balances 69

Be wary of scams and phishing attempts 69
- Awareness Training 69
- Vigilance and Skepticism 70
- Hygienic Security Measures 70
- Reporting and Response 71

Keep your software and devices updated 71
- Maintenance of Patches 71
- Automatic Content Updates 72

Scanning for vulnerabilities 72
- Configuring the Security System 72

Avoid risking too much 73
- Assessment of the Risk 73
- Strategic Approach to Diversification 74
- Fund for Emergencies 74
- Perspectives on Investment 74

Stay updated on market trends and news 75
- Analysis of the Market: 75
- Sources of the News 76
- Schedule of Events 76
- Engagement with the Community 77

Consider consulting a professional 77
- Financial Advisor 77
- Consultant for Taxes 78

- Legal Advisor _____ 78
- Associations of Professionals _____ 79

The advantages and disadvantages of using cryptocurrency _____ 79

Advantages of Cryptocurrency _____ 80

Transaction speed _____ 81

Protection from inflation _____ 82

Cost-effective transactions _____ 83

A decentralized system _____ 84

Accessibility _____ 86

Protection and safety _____ 87

Transparency _____ 88

Confidentiality _____ 90

Easy currency exchange _____ 91

Disadvantages of Cryptocurrency _____ 92

Pseudonymous transactions _____ 93

Constant risk of an attack _____ 94

Excessive power consumption _____ 95

Lack of key policies _____ 96

Costly network participation _____ 97

CHAPTER 5 _____ 99

Getting Started with Crypto Trading _____ 99

Different kinds of cryptocurrency wallets _____ 100

Software wallet _____ 101

Creating a software wallet _____ 101

Hardware wallets _____ 103

A hardware wallet can be set up in the following manner _____ 104

- Purchase the device 104
- Download the software 104
- Connect your device 105
- Add cryptocurrency to your wallet 106
- Custodial wallet 106
  - Setting up a custodial crypto wallet 107
    - Find a trustworthy platform 107
    - Sign up for an account. 107
    - Add cryptocurrency to your wallet 108
- A Guide to Purchasing Cryptocurrency 109
  - Stages involved in purchasing cryptocurrency 110
    - Typical brokers and dealers 110
    - Cryptocurrency exchanges 111
- Alternative methods of investing in cryptocurrency 114
  - Bitcoin trusts 115
  - Bitcoin mutual funds 115
  - Blockchain stocks or ETFs 115

CHAPTER 6 117

Introduction to Technical Analysis 117
- Key Components of Crypto Technical Analysis 118
  - Price action 119
  - Cryptocurrency charts 119
  - Volume 120
  - Market trends 120
  - Technical Indicators 121
- Chart Patterns and Trend Analysis for Cryptocurrency 121

- Cryptocurrency Chart Patterns ... 122
  - Head and Shoulders ... 122
  - Double Top ... 122
  - Triangle patterns ... 123
- Trend Analysis ... 123
  - Bullish ... 123
  - Bearish ... 123
  - Consolidation ... 123
- Importance of Volume and Volatility in Crypto Technical Analysis ... 124
  - Understanding volume in cryptocurrency ... 125
  - Volatility in Cryptocurrency Technical Analysis ... 126
- Technical Indicators and Their Importance in Crypto-analysis ... 127
  - Understanding the various types of technical indicators ... 127
    - Trend Indicators ... 128
    - Momentum indicators ... 128
    - Volatility Indicators ... 129
    - Volume indicators ... 129
- Common Pitfalls in Crypto Technical Analysis ... 130
  - Overconfidence with Technical Analysis Tools ... 130
  - Disregard Market News and Events ... 131
  - Incorrect use of technical indicators ... 131
  - Lack of a structured trading plan ... 132

CHAPTER ONE

An overview of cryptocurrencies

The term cryptocurrency refers to a digital currency, which is an alternate approach to payment that is developed through the use of encryption techniques. Cryptocurrencies are able to perform the functions of both a conventional money and a digital accounting system because they make use of encryption technologies.

It is necessary to have a cryptocurrency wallet in order to use cryptocurrencies. These wallets can be software that is an online service that is hosted in the cloud, or they can be saved on your personal computer or mobile device.

The wallets are the pieces of software that you use to store your encryption keys, which are used to verify your identity and establish a connection to your bitcoin.

Operations of cryptocurrency

There is a distributed public ledger known as blockchain that is used to run cryptocurrencies. This ledger is a record of all transactions that are updated and retained by currency holders.

A process known as mining is responsible for the creation of units of cryptocurrency. This process requires the utilization of computer power to solve complex mathematical problems that result in the generation of coins.

Additionally, users have the option of purchasing the currencies from brokers, storing them in encrypted wallets, and then spending them.

In the case of bitcoin ownership, you do not possess any physical assets.

Rather than relying on a third party, you can transfer records or units of measurement directly between yourself and another individual using the key that you hold.

In spite of the fact that Bitcoin has been there since 2009, cryptocurrencies and applications of block-chain technology are still in the process of emerging in the financial sector, and it is anticipated that additional applications will emerge in the future.

At some point in the future, the technology will be able to facilitate the trading of financial assets such as stocks, bonds, and other financial instruments.

The trading of cryptocurrencies is a highly speculative and complicated endeavor that carries a substantial amount of risk. It is possible for prices to change on any given day.

Because of the constant price fluctuations, cryptocurrency is only appropriate for certain types of investors.

Because of this, cryptocurrency ought to be regarded as an investment with a high level of risk. Obtain a financial advisor's advice and make sure you are aware of the potential dangers before you invest.

Numerous Advantages of Cryptocurrency

Unlike, for instance, the fee that is charged for transferring money from a digital wallet to a bank account, the transaction cost associated with cryptocurrencies is extremely low, and in some cases it is even nonexistent.

Transactions can be made at any time of the day or night, and there are no restrictions placed on the amount of money that can be withdrawn or purchased. In contrast to the process of opening a bank account, which necessitates the submission of documentation and other paperwork, the use of Bitcoin is open to anybody.

Not only are international cryptocurrency transactions quicker than wire transfers, but they are also faster. The time it takes for money to go from one location to another through the use of wire transfers is around half a day. Transactions involving cryptocurrency can be completed in a couple of minutes or even seconds.

Some examples of cryptocurrencies

There is a vast number of cryptocurrencies available. Among the most well-known are the following:

Bitcoin

Bitcoin, which was established in 2009, is the first cryptocurrency and continues to be the most widely traded cryptocurrency.

Satoshi Nakamoto, who is commonly thought to be a pseudonym for an individual or group of persons whose precise identity remains unknown, is the person who is credited with developing the currency.

Ethereum

Ethereum is a blockchain platform that includes its own cryptocurrency, which is referred to as Ether (ETH) or Ethereum. It was developed in the year 2015. Following Bitcoin in popularity, it is the most widely used cryptocurrency.

Litecoin

The most striking similarity between this money and bitcoin is that it has advanced more rapidly in terms of the development of new innovations, such as speedier payment processes and procedures that enable more transactions.

Ripples

2012 marked the beginning of Ripple, a distributed ledger system that was established. Ripple is not limited to tracking cryptocurrency transactions; it may also be used to track other types of transactions. A number of banks and other financial institutions have been clients of the company that is responsible for it.

Those cryptocurrencies that are not Bitcoin are referred to collectively as "altcoins" in order to differentiate them from the original Bitcoin.

CHAPTER TWO

Cryptocurrency scams and security

Regrettably, criminal activity involving cryptocurrencies is on the rise. Some examples of cryptocurrency frauds are:

Fraudulent websites

Assuming that you continue to invest, fraudulent websites that showcase fabricated testimonials and crypto jargon promise big profits that are not reliable.

Online Ponzi schemes

Those who engage in criminal activity involving cryptocurrencies promote chances to invest in digital currencies that do not exist and create the idea of enormous returns by paying off previous investors with the money of new investors. More than 700 million dollars was raised by one fraudulent enterprise known as BitClub Network before the perpetrators of the scheme were indicted in December of 2019.

Endorsements from famous people

Swindlers will masquerade as billionaires or well-known individuals on the internet and make the promise that they will multiply your investment in a virtual currency. However, they will steal what you pay them instead. It is also possible for them to use messaging applications or chat rooms in order to spread the theory that a well-known businessperson is supporting a particular cryptocurrency. After they have succeeded in luring investors to purchase and driving up the price, the con artists will then sell their interest, which will result in a decrease in the value of the currency.

Romance scams

When it comes to online dating scams, the Federal Bureau of Investigation (FBI) is warning of a trend in which con artists convince people they meet on dating apps or social media to invest or trade in virtual currencies. A total of more than 1,800 reports of crypto-focused romantic scams were received by the Internet Crime Complaint Centre of the Federal Bureau of Investigation during the first seven months of 2021, with losses reaching a total of $133 million.

Under any other circumstances, con artists may pose as legitimate dealers of virtual currencies or establish fake exchanges in order to deceive individuals into giving them money. One such type of fraudulent activity involving cryptocurrencies is the use of fraudulent sales pitches for individual retirement accounts in cryptocurrency.

Then there is the straightforward form of cryptocurrency hacking, which involves thieves breaking into digital wallets with the intention of stealing the virtual currency that individuals have stored in those wallets.

Is it safe to use cryptocurrency

The blockchain technology is typically utilized in the construction of cryptocurrencies. The term "blockchain" refers to the transactional process of recording transactions into "blocks" and time stamping them. Despite the fact that it is a very complicated and technical procedure, the end result is a digital record of cryptocurrency transactions that is difficult for hackers to manipulate.

Moreover, a two-factor authentication procedure is necessary for the completion of transactions.

In order to initiate a transaction, for instance, you might be required to provide a username and a password simultaneously. It is possible that you will be required to provide an authentication code that has been sent to your personal cell phone via text message.

Despite the fact that there are safeguards in place, this does not mean that cryptocurrencies are impossible to hack. Cryptocurrency start-ups have suffered significant losses as a result of multiple high-dollar thefts. The hacking of Coincheck, which resulted in a loss of $534 million, and BitGrail, which gained $195 million, are two of the most significant cryptocurrency attacks that occurred in 2018.

The value of virtual currencies is solely determined by supply and demand, in contrast to the value of money that is backed by the government. In this way, large swings can occur, which can result in significant gains for investors or significant losses for them.

Additionally, investments in cryptocurrencies are subject to a far lower level of regulatory protection compared to traditional financial instruments such as equities, bonds, and mutual funds among others.

Cryptocurrency security

Cryptography

Cryptography is a technique that involves the use of encryption and decryption in order to ensure the safety of communication in the presence of third parties who have malicious intentions.

These third parties may be interested in stealing your data or listening in on your conversation. Cryptography makes use of computational techniques such as SHA-256, which is the hashing algorithm that Bitcoin employs; a public key, which is analogous to a digital identity of the user that is shared with everyone; and a private key, which is a digital signature of the user that is kept concealed.

The field of cryptocurrency relies heavily on cryptography as a fundamental mathematical notion. The practice and study of methods for ensuring the confidentiality of communication in the presence of third parties, who are frequently referred to as adversaries, is what this term refers to. When it comes to the realm of cryptocurrency, cryptography is an extremely important factor in preserving the confidentiality, integrity, and security of data and transactions with bitcoin.

Here are some of the most important features of the relationship between cryptography and cryptocurrency:

Transaction Security

Through the use of cryptography, cryptocurrency networks are able to guarantee the safety and immutability of their transactions. Through the use of the sender's private key, each transaction is digitally signed. This serves to authenticate the transaction and assures that only the rightful owner of the cryptocurrency can initiate transactions.

Cryptographic algorithms such as ECDSA (Elliptic Curve Digital Signature Algorithm) and RSA (Rivest-Shamir-Adleman) are utilized in the process of generating digital signatures. These algorithms offer robust security assurances against the unauthorized modification or forgery of transactions.

Cryptography based on public keys:

Pairs of keys are utilized in public key cryptography, which is also referred to as asymmetric cryptography. For example, a public key and a private key are used.

On the other hand, the private key is kept a secret and is utilized for decryption or signature, while the public key is made available to the public and is utilized for encryption or verification.

Cryptography with public keys is utilized in the cryptocurrency industry to generate addresses for the purpose of receiving cash. It is possible to generate a pseudonymous identification for the user by using the public address, which is generated from the public key. Concurrently, the private key is utilized for the purpose of signing transactions and demonstrating possession of cash.

Hash Functions

Cryptographic hash functions are mathematical functions that only produce a single output (hash) from an arbitrary input.

These functions are one-way functions. It is computationally impossible to reverse-engineer the input from the output since they are designed to be irreversible and fast to compute. This means that they are designed to be fast to compute.

Hash functions are utilized in the cryptocurrency industry for a variety of purposes, including the generation of transaction IDs, which are unique identifiers for transactions, the creation of blocks in blockchain networks, and the provision of the foundation for proof-of-work algorithms, such as Bitcoin's SHA-256 algorithm.

By generating one-of-a-kind fingerprints for each piece of data, hash functions guarantee the data's integrity. Modifications or tampering can be easily identified since even a slight adjustment in the data that is supplied results in a hash that is drastically different from the one that is generated.

Encryption

It is the process of converting plaintext into ciphertext through the utilization of cryptographic algorithms and keys that constitute encryption. The confidentiality of sensitive information is maintained, and it is rendered unreadable to individuals who are not allowed to view it.

Within the realm of cryptocurrency, encryption serves the purpose of safeguarding the contents of wallets and ensuring the security of communication channels (for example, SSL/TLS encryption for network communications). In order to prevent unauthorized access to private keys and other sensitive data, wallets frequently encrypt these contents.

For the purpose of protecting cryptocurrency transactions and data, advanced encryption methods such as Advanced Encryption Standard (AES) and Elliptic Curve Cryptography (ECC) are frequently utilized.

Digital Signatures

Using digital signatures, one may demonstrate the validity, integrity, and non-repudiation of digital messages or transactions. This process is known as digital signature verification.

Application of cryptographic algorithms to transaction data using the sender's private key is the process that results in the creation of digital signatures in the cryptocurrency industry. The signature that is generated is added to the transaction, and it is possible for anyone to verify it by using the public key obtained from the sender.

The use of digital signatures guarantees that financial transactions are authorized in a safe manner and will not be amended without rendering the signature invalid. They are an essential component of the trustless nature of cryptocurrency networks, which eliminates the requirement for intermediaries or trusted third parties to validate transactions.

CHAPTER THREE

A Guide to Block-chain Technology

Block-chain is a cutting-edge database technology that serves as the foundation for almost all cryptocurrencies. Through the use of block-chain technology, which involves the distribution of identical copies of a database throughout an entire network, it becomes extremely impossible to hack or cheat the system.

How Does Block-chain Work

A block-chain is a digital ledger that cannot be altered and helps to ensure the safety of transactions that take place via a peer-to-peer network.

It eliminates the need for third parties, such as banks or governments, by simultaneously recording, storing, and verifying data through the utilization of decentralized mechanisms.

The block-chain is a distributed ledger that records each transaction and then stores it in a block. Each block is encrypted for the purpose of providing protection, and it is chained to the block that came before it (thus the term "block-chain"), which establishes a chronological sequence based on the code.

This indicates that data that is kept on a block-chain cannot be erased or modified unless there is a consensus among the network's participants. In addition to serving as a single source of truth, these modern databases, which are distributed throughout a network of interconnected computers, make it possible to share data in a trustworthy and transparent manner.

Block-chain technology is a developing technology that has the potential to be applied in a broad variety of contexts, including the prevention of fraudulent banking and supply-chain bottlenecks, the protection of medical information, and the transfer of cryptocurrency from one wallet to another.

Significance of block-chain technology

Because it helps decrease security concerns, eliminate fraud, and deliver transparency in a scalable manner, block-chain is a technology that is going to revolutionize the cryptocurrency industry.

After initially gaining popularity due to its link with cryptocurrencies and non-fungible tokens (NFTs), block-chain technology has subsequently developed into a management solution that can be utilized by a wide variety of worldwide enterprises.

Block-chain technology is currently being used to provide transparency for the food supply chain, to secure healthcare data, to innovate games, and to change the way that we handle data and ownership on a big scale.

The operations of block-chain technology

The distributed data management systems known as block-chains are able to record each and every transaction that takes place between their members. A trustless and intermediary-free system is created through the utilization of a number of different ways by these immutable digital documents.

The blocks, Known as a hash, each block is comprised of data that has been stored, in addition to its own one-of-a-kind alphanumeric code. A digital fingerprint is a term that can be used to describe these codes that are generated by cryptography.

The fact that new blocks are formed from the hash code of the previous block, so producing a chronological sequence and providing tamper proofing, is one of the ways in which they contribute to the connecting of blocks together. Every change that is made to these codes results in the output of a completely different string of gibberish, which makes it simple for participants to identify and reject blocks that do not fit the pattern.

The decentralized nature of block-chain technology is yet another essential component of its inner workings.

Block-chain technology eliminates the need for a central authority by distributing control throughout a peer-to-peer network that is comprised of nodes, which are computers that are connected to one another. Keeping the digital ledger up to date is the responsibility of these nodes, which are in continual communication with one another.

At the time that a transaction is taking place between two peers, all of the nodes in the network participate in the process of validating the transaction by utilizing consensus methods. Because of these built-in protocols, all of the nodes in the network are able to reach a consensus on a single data set.

It is not possible to add blocks to the block-chain until verification and consensus have been obtained on the block-chain. In a fortunate turn of events, this stage has been accelerated thanks to the introduction of smart contracts. Smart contracts are self-executing programs that are written into a block-chain and automate the verification process.

When a transaction is documented, it is assumed to be regarded permanent. Because there are no activities that can be reversed, block-chains are considered to be one-way operations.

A trustworthy record of all activity on the block-chain is created by the immutability of the block-chain, which contributes to the creation of transparency across the network.

Block-chain Decentralization

The concept of decentralization is at the forefront of block-chain technology and is considered to be critical. In no way can the chain be owned by a single computer or entity.

On the contrary, it functions as a distributed ledger through the nodes that are connected to the chain. The term "block-chain node" refers to any type of electronic device that is responsible for maintaining copies of the chain and ensuring that the network performs its functions.

Each node has a copy of the block-chain, and in order for the chain to be updated, trusted, and validated, the network must algorithmically approve each newly mined block.

On account of the fact that block-chains are transparent, any action that takes place in the ledger can be easily examined and viewed, which results in the inherent security of block-chains.

Each participant is provided with a one-of-a-kind identifying number consisting of letters and numbers that displays their transactions.

The block-chain is able to maintain its integrity and foster confidence among its users when public information is combined with a system of checks and balances. In its most basic form, block-chains can be conceptualized as the scalability of trust through the use of technology.

Benefits of Block-chain

A Higher Level of Safety

In order to guarantee that only authorized users are able to access information that is intended for them, cryptography and hashing techniques are utilized.

Additionally, the data that is kept on the block-chain is secured against any kind of manipulation. By requiring network participants to reach a consensus on the legitimacy of transactions before they are added to the block-chain, consensus methods, like as proof of work or proof of stake, further strengthen the level of security that is present in the block-chain.

It is also important to note that block-chains function on a distributed basis, which means that data is stored among numerous nodes rather than in a single central location. This eliminates the possibility of a single point of failure occurring.

Enhancement of Accuracy

The chance for error or inconsistency is reduced as compared to centralized databases or manual record-keeping systems. This is accomplished by providing a ledger that is completely visible and serves as a single source of truth.

Transactions are recorded in a chronological and unchangeable way. Unless a block-chain is made secret, all transactions may be independently verified by users.

Transactions are objectively authorized by a consensus mechanism, and users have the ability to verify all transactions independently.

Increased Productivity and Efficiency

Not only does block-chain save paper, but it also makes it possible for teams to communicate with one another in a trustworthy manner, lowers bottlenecks and errors, and streamlines processes overall.

Block-chain features reduced transaction costs, quick processing times, and optimized data integrity. This is made possible by the elimination of intermediaries and the automation of verification processes, which are accomplished through the use of smart contracts.

Block-chain related challenges

Despite the fact that this developing technology may be impervious to manipulation, it is not without flaws. The following are some of the most significant challenges that block-chain technology is now facing.

Restrictions on Transactions

These block-chain networks are experiencing limitations in their ability to conduct transactions in a timely and cost-effective manner as their popularity and usage continue to expand. As a result of this constraint, the widespread adoption of block-chain technology for mainstream applications is hampered.

This is because networks struggle to handle high throughput levels, which results in congestion and increasing transaction costs.

The Consumption of Energy

Certain operations, such as Bitcoin's proof-of-work consensus process, need a significant amount of computational power, which results in the use of enormous amounts of electricity.

This raises worries regarding the impact on the environment as well as the high expenses of operation. In order to address this difficulty, it is necessary to investigate alternate consensus techniques, such as proof of stake, which consume a substantially lower amount of energy while still preserving the decentralization and security of the network.

Problems with Scalability

In the current state of affairs, each node that makes up a block-chain network is responsible for processing each transaction and storing a copy of the whole data chain.

This necessitates a certain amount of computer capacity, which leads to slow, crowded networks and sluggish processing times, particularly during times of high traffic volume.

Scalability problems develop as a result of restrictions on block size, processing durations for blocks, and consensus procedures that require a significant amount of resources.

Concerns Regarding Regulation

There is still a lot of work to be done by governments and regulators in order to make sense of block-chain technology. More specifically, they are discussing how certain laws should be modified in order to appropriately accommodate decentralization.

The market attractiveness of block-chain technology is hindered by persisting regulatory and legal issues, which in turn halts the development of its technical capabilities. While some governments are actively leading the way in its adoption, others have chosen to wait and watch.

Applications and Use Cases of Block-chain Technology

Block-chain was initially developed as a means of ensuring the integrity of digital information by utilizing technology that is resistant to tampering.

In the time that has passed since the introduction of the data management protocol into the mainstream alongside the introduction of Bitcoin, it has extended beyond the realm of DeFi and into its many businesses across a wide range of applications.

Banks and lenders

The use of block-chain technology makes it simpler for financial institutions to exchange currencies, obtain loans, and process payments.

This piece of technology functions as a single-layer, source-of-truth that is intended to monitor each and every transaction that its users have ever carried out. Because of this immutability, fraud in the banking industry is prevented, which results in speedier settlement times.

Additionally, it serves as an integrated monitor for money laundering. Banks also gain from international transactions that are completed more quickly and at lower prices, as well as from high-security data encryption.

Smart Contracts

Transaction verification can be automated with the help of smart contracts, which are protocols that execute themselves. The block-chain is used to encode them, and the terms that govern them are predetermined.

Not only do they help to reduce the amount of errors that are caused by humans, but they also help to enable decentralization and create an environment that is trustless by taking the place of third-party intermediaries.

Cyber security

Block-chain's decentralized, tamper-proof record, dubbed a "new weapon in cybersecurity," includes built-in defenses against theft, fraud, and unauthorized users through cryptographic coding and consensus procedures. In light of this, block-chain technology has been included into cybersecurity arsenals for the purpose of preserving bitcoin, protecting bank assets, safeguarding patient health information, strengthening Internet of Things devices, and even protecting data from the military and defense sector.

Medical care

Block-chain technology is mostly utilized by healthcare providers for the purpose of encrypting patient data that is maintained in their medical records. Certain functions, such as smart contracts, automate activities such as the filing of insurance claims and the monitoring of medication adherence, which results in an increase in efficiency and a reduction in administrative overhead.

Block-chain technology not only makes it easier for healthcare professionals, patients, and researchers to safely share medical information with one another, but it is also being utilized by genome-sequencing firms in order to assist in the process of deciphering the genetic code.

The logistics

Block-chain technology serves as a track-and-trace tool in the logistics industry, allowing for the tracking of the movement of items along the supply chain. The open-source system provides users with the ability to monitor their shipments in real time, from the point of manufacture to the point of delivery.

These realizations assist in the compilation of data, the determination of speedier routes, the elimination of unneeded middlemen, and even the defense against interference from cyberattacks.

NFTs

When it comes to non-fungible tokens, or NFTs, block-chain technology enables the creation, ownership, and trade of these tokens.

The fact that each non-fungible token (NFT) is encrypted with block-chain technology, which maintains a live running record of ownership over the piece, is the reason why copying these digital assets is not as simple as taking a quick screenshot. Transactions are governed by smart contracts, which ensure that ownership is assigned and reassigned, and that royalties are distributed to artists as items are transferred from one wallet to another.

Different types of block-chain

In tandem with the development of block-chain technology, additional variants have emerged. In this part, a quick introduction is given to four distinct models that have developed as a result of demand.

Public block-chain

Public block-chains are networks that do not require additional permissions and are regarded to be "fully decentralized." Users are able to maintain their anonymity while using the distributed ledger, which is not controlled by any one company or individual. It is possible for a user to take part in the network so long as they are able to give evidence of their effort.

Private block-chain

Permissioned networks are considered to be private block-chains. For the purpose of achieving a higher level of control or privacy over a network, private block-chains are managed by a single operator who is responsible for determining who is permitted to access the network and whether or not members are able to view, verify, or generate data on the block-chain.

The addition of restricted access to an encrypted record-keeping ledger is appealing to certain businesses that work with sensitive information, such as large corporations or government agencies.

Consortium Block-chain

Consortium block-chains, which are often referred to as federated block-chains, are defined as permissioned networks that are managed by a particular group of individuals.

There are multiple users who have the ability to modify or cancel transactions, as well as create the rules. If the block-chain is designed with shared authority, it may be able to achieve higher levels of both efficiency and anonymity.

Hybrid Block-chain

Block-chains that make use of hybrid technology integrate aspects of both public and private networks.

They have a feature called selective transparency, which enables the administrators of the block-chain to restrict certain parts of the block-chain to particular participant pools while still allowing the public to view the remainder of the thread. In this manner, companies have the right to a certain degree of privacy when they are sharing data in an unchangeable manner without the involvement of a third party.

A Brief History of Block-chain

The origin of block-chain is generally attributed to David Chaum, a cryptography professor. Chaum first described a protocol that was similar to block-chain among a decentralized node network in a dissertation that he submitted in 1982. The first indications of it, on the other hand, date all the way back to the 1970s, when computer scientist Ralph Merkle developed hash trees, which are often referred to as Merkle trees. These trees enable cryptographic linkage between blocks of data that have been stored.

When the very first block-chain product was introduced in 1991, these theories would finally come together to form a coherent whole. Stuart Haber, a scientist, and Scott Stornetta, a cryptographer, collaborated on the development of a computational solution that would time-stamp documents using a hash function in a chronological chain of digital certificates.

This was done in an effort to establish records that are tamper-proof in the digital era. Merkle trees were included into the architecture the next year, with the assistance of the mathematician David Bayer. This allowed for the consolidation of data into a single block, which is comparable to the functionality that we are familiar with in block-chain technology today.

Then, in 2009, Bitcoin, the very first cryptocurrency ever created, was introduced to the public.

The peer-to-peer electronic cash system, which was launched under the pseudonym Satoshi Nakamoto, not only offered a digital alternative to fiat currency, but it also introduced the concept of a public, decentralized block-chain that eliminates the need for intervention by a third party.

This initiative was significantly responsible for integrating block-chain into our everyday lexicon, and it wasn't until 2015, when the Ethereum platform was launched, that it was successfully challenged by another project.

Smart contracts, which are self-executing programs that automate transaction verification, and decentralized applications, often known as DApps, which enable developers to participate in Web3 by building their own applications, are two ways that Vitalik Buterin, the architect of block-chain technology, is advancing the technology.

And despite the fact that block-chain is almost synonymous with Web3 and bitcoin, the distributed ledger technology has made its way into a variety of industries in the twenty years that have passed since its first deployment in the real world. These businesses include alleviating bottlenecks in the shipping process and delivering transparent patient care respectively.

CHAPTER FOUR

Cryptocurrency investment opportunities

Although Consumer Reports asserts that every investment carries some degree of risk, there are some financial professionals who believe that cryptocurrency is among the most risky investment options currently available. These suggestions can assist you in making well-informed decisions if you are considering making an investment in cryptocurrencies.

Investing in Cryptocurrency: Some Safeguards to Consider

Education and Research

- Components of Block-chain:

Get familiar with the essential ideas behind block-chain technology, such as its decentralized nature, the methods that facilitate consensus, and the cryptographic security characteristics that it possesses.

- Having an Understanding of Cryptocurrency:

Explore the particulars of a number of different cryptocurrencies, such as Bitcoin, Ethereum, and other alternative cryptocurrencies, in greater depth. The underlying technologies, distinctive qualities, and prospective applications of their product should be investigated.

- Analysis of the Market:

To get a comprehensive understanding of the market trends, historical price data, trading volume, and market capitalization of various cryptocurrencies, you need conduct extensive study. Consider aspects such as the rate of adoption, the support of the community, and the amount of development activities.

- Assessment of the Risk:

Take into consideration the dangers that are connected with investing in cryptocurrencies, such as the volatility of the market, the unpredictability of regulatory policies, and the vulnerabilities of the technology. Before you make any decisions, you should think about your level of comfort with risk and your investment goals.

- Useful Resources for Education:

For the purpose of enhancing your knowledge and comprehension of the cryptocurrency market, you should make use of a wide range of educational resources, including online courses, books, webinars, and cryptocurrency forums.

Make sure to use reliable exchanges

- Security Features:

It is important to evaluate the security mechanisms that cryptocurrency exchanges have put into place, such as encryption techniques, cold storage solutions, and multi-signature wallets. Keep an eye out for exchanges that put the safety and privacy of their users first.

- Complying with the Regulations:

It is imperative that you verify that the exchange satisfies all applicable regulatory criteria and possesses all of the necessary licenses and certificates. If you want to avoid larger dangers, you should steer clear of unregulated or offshore markets.

- Trading Volume and Liquidity:

It is important to take into consideration the trading volume and liquidity of the exchange, as a higher level of liquidity makes it easier to execute deals more quickly and decreases slippage.

- User Experience:

Conduct an analysis of the user interface, trading tools, and customer support services that are provided by the electronic exchange.

Determine which platforms are user-friendly and offer complete support to users, then select those platforms.

- Reputation in the Community:

Investigation on the reliability and repute of the exchange within the bitcoin community should be carried out. To get a sense of what other users' experiences were like, read reviews, testimonials, and feedback from other users.

Diversify the investments you have

- Distribution of Assets:

In order to create a diverse investment portfolio, you should distribute your funds among a variety of cryptocurrencies.

These cryptocurrencies should include well-known coins such as Bitcoin and Ethereum, as well as promising alternative cryptocurrencies that provide distinctive value propositions.

- The Management of Risk:

Reduce the impact of risk by spreading your investment among a number of different assets, each of which has a unique risk profile. Make sure you don't have an excessive exposure to any one cryptocurrency or asset type.

- The Rebalancing of Portfolios:

It is important to ensure that your investment portfolio is regularly reviewed and rebalanced in accordance with the shifting market conditions, performance indicators, and investment objectives.

Your allocation should be adjusted so that you can keep the ideal balance between risk and reward.

- Long-Term Perspective:

When making investments, it is important to adopt a long-term view and concentrate on projects that have solid fundamentals, active development teams, and sustainable growth possibilities. It is important to refrain from either seeking short-term benefits or giving in to FOMO (fear of missing out).

Use hardware wallets for long-term storage

- **Cold Storage Solutions:**

Protect your cryptocurrency assets by putting a sizeable amount of your funds in hardware wallets, which are offline devices designed to safely store private keys. This will ensure that your bitcoin holdings are protected.

- **Security Features:**

Choose hardware wallets that include extensive security features like as password encryption, personal identification number (PIN) protection, and designs that are resistant to tampering. It is important to confirm the device's legitimacy and make certain that it has not been altered in any way.

- **Procedures for Backing Up:**

It is important to have comprehensive backup methods in place in order to protect your hardware wallet from being lost or stolen. It is important to keep backup seeds or recovery phrases in safe places, such as safety deposit boxes or encrypted storage devices.

- Perform Routine Maintenance:

Maintaining the firmware of your hardware wallet with regular updates will ensure that it is equipped with the most recent security patches and bug fixes. Maintaining the equipment in accordance with best practices and performing frequent tests to ensure its integrity are both important.

Enable two-factor authentication (2FA)

- Stronger Safety Measures:

Implementing two-factor authentication, also known as 2FA, on all of your cryptocurrency exchange accounts, wallets, and online platforms will provide an additional layer of security in addition to the passwords you use.

- Techniques for Authentication:

Two-factor authentication can be accomplished through a variety of means, such as text message authentication, authenticator apps (such as Google Authenticator and Authy), hardware tokens, or biometric verification. Based on your preferences, choose the one that offers the highest level of safety and convenience.

- Codes for backups:

If you find yourself unable to access your primary authentication method, it is important to generate backup codes or recovery keys for two-factor authentication and store them in a secure location. Make sure that backup codes are stored in a safe place, such as a password manager or a file that includes encryption.

- Checks and Balances:

Conduct regular audits and reviews of your two-factor authentication settings to verify that they are always up to current and configured correctly. All unused authentication methods should be disabled or removed, and access should be revoked for any devices or apps that are not allowed.

Be wary of scams and phishing attempts

- Awareness Training:

Make sure that you and the other members of your team are aware of the often encountered cryptocurrency scams, phishing techniques, and social engineering strategies that are utilized by bad actors.

- Vigilance and Skepticism:

In the event that you get unsolicited emails, texts, or social media postings that promote investment opportunities, initial coin offerings (ICOs), airdrops, or giveaways, you should exercise caution and skepticism. Performing due diligence and confirming the sender's validity are both necessary steps before taking any action.

- Hygienic Security Measures:

It is important to maintain excellent security hygiene by utilizing robust and one-of-a-kind passwords for your accounts, setting spam filters and email authentication methods, and avoiding clicking on questionable links or downloading files from unfamiliar sources.

- Reporting and Response:

Phishing attempts, fraudulent actions, and suspicious conduct should be reported to the appropriate authorities, regulatory agencies, or cybersecurity organizations with the appropriate information. When you think that your accounts and assets have been compromised or accessed without authorization, you should take fast measures to secure them.

Keep your software and devices updated

- Maintenance of Patches:

It is important to ensure that the software, firmware, and operating systems of your devices, including as computers, smartphones, tablets, and hardware wallets, are regularly updated in order to address any known vulnerabilities and reduce the potential for security breaches.

- Automatic Content Updates:

To guarantee that your devices receive the most recent software updates and security patches without requiring any intervention from you, it is important to enable automatic updates wherever it is possible to do so.

Scanning for vulnerabilities

Make use of vulnerability scanning tools and security software in order to locate and fix any potential security flaws that may exist in your systems and apps. In order to proactively resolve any security gaps, it is important to do regular scans and assessments.

- Configuring the Security System:

Your devices and applications should have their security settings and privacy controls configured in order to provide a higher level of protection against malicious software, phishing attacks, and unwanted access. It is recommended that encryption, firewall protection, and intrusion detection technologies be enabled to the proper extent.

Avoid risking too much

- Assessment of the Risk:

Before investing money in cryptocurrencies, you should first evaluate your current financial condition, your level of comfort with risk, and your investment goals.

You should only invest money that you can afford to lose without it having a negative influence on your long-term goals or your capacity to maintain your financial stability.

- Strategic Approach to Diversification:

Take advantage of a diversified investment plan that allows you to diversify your risk over a variety of asset types, such as real estate, equities, bonds, and cryptocurrencies. It is important to avoid putting all of your eggs in one basket and to keep your portfolio well-balanced.

- Fund for Emergencies:

It is important to keep a cash reserve or emergency fund in order to handle any unexpected bills, crises, or temporary setbacks that may arise.

It is important to make the establishment of a financial safety net a top priority before investing money in speculative assets such as cryptocurrency.

- Perspectives on Investment:

Consider your financial objectives, your level of comfort with risk, and the stage of your life when determining your investment horizon and time horizon.

When preparing your investing strategy, it is important to take into consideration the potential liquidity limits, volatility, and cyclical changes that are associated with the cryptocurrency market.

Stay updated on market trends and news

Analysis of the Market:
In order to detect new opportunities and risks in the cryptocurrency market, it is important to continuously watch market trends, price fluctuations, trading volumes, and sentiment indicators. When making decisions about investments, it is important to make use of tools that provide technical analysis, fundamental analysis, and sentiment analysis.

- Sources of the News:

Maintain a level of awareness on the most recent news, announcements, regulatory changes, and industry trends all of which have an impact on the bitcoin market.

To ensure that you are always up to date with the most recent information, it is important to follow credible news sites, blogs, forums, social media channels, and cryptocurrency influencers.

- Schedule of Events:

Maintain a thorough awareness of forthcoming events, conferences, product launches, protocol upgrades, and regulatory notifications that have the potential to impact the dynamics of the market and the sentiment of investors. You should keep a calendar that contains important dates and milestones that are associated with your financial portfolio.

- Engagement with the Community:

Maintain an active presence within the cryptocurrency ecosystem by participating in online forums, discussion groups, and social media communities.

This will allow you to interact with other investors, share ideas, and share observations. Enjoy the opportunity to take part in live events, webinars, and AMAs (Ask Me Anything) sessions that are hosted by thought leaders and industry professionals.

Consider consulting a professional

- Financial Advisor:

You should discuss your investing goals, your level of comfort with risk, and your current financial circumstances with a certified financial counselor, investment strategist, or wealth manager.

You should look for individualized advice and direction that is customized to your particular requirements and goals.

- Consultant for Taxes:

To successfully manage the intricate tax ramifications that are associated with your investment activities, it is recommended that you seek the assistance of a tax consultant or a certified public accountant (CPA) who specializes in cryptocurrency taxation. Keep yourself in compliance with the many tax laws, reporting obligations, and regulatory norms that are applicable.

- Legal Advisor:

Consult with seasoned attorneys or other legal professionals who specialize in cryptocurrency law, regulatory compliance, and investor protection in order to obtain legal counsel and direction. Make sure that the activities you engage in regarding investments are in accordance with the applicable laws, regulations, and contractual responsibilities.

- **Associations of Professionals:**

Establish connections with professionals, experts, and industry insiders who are involved in the bitcoin ecosystem. These individuals may include developers, researchers, analysts, and entrepreneurs. Utilize their expertise, insights, and networks to your advantage in order to acquire access to valuable resources, opportunities, and strategic alliances.

The advantages and disadvantages of using cryptocurrency

Cryptocurrency is a topic that elicits heated comments from investment professionals across the board.

Listed below are a few of the reasons why other individuals are concerned that it is just a passing fad, while others believe that it is a revolutionary technology.

Advantages of Cryptocurrency

There are many advantages associated with cryptocurrency, including increased security, accessibility on a worldwide scale, transparency, and reduced transaction fees.

On the other hand, it does not come without any drawbacks, such as high price fluctuation, a lack of regulation, technical limitations for certain users, and the possibility of misuse.

Pros and cons of cryptocurrency are the characteristics that collectively determine the risk and reward profile of digital currency investments. These factors represent the pros and cons of cryptocurrency.

Below are the detailed advantages of cryptocurrency.

Transaction speed

When we talk about the speed of transactions, we are referring to the rate at which a financial transaction, such as a transfer or payment, can be finished. Due to the many checks and procedures that are involved, overseas transactions made through traditional banking may take several days to complete.

Because of cryptocurrencies, the pace at which transactions are completed is frequently significantly faster. Transactions involving cryptocurrencies can be processed in a matter of minutes or even seconds because to the decentralized technology involved in Block-chain. The speed of this process makes it possible to make instantaneous global transactions without the need for intermediaries or extended periods of waiting.

However, the speed may vary depending on the cryptocurrency utilized and network congestion at the time of the transaction, causing the real timings to fluctuate.

Protection from inflation

The ability of certain assets, including certain cryptocurrencies, to provide protection against inflation is a significant advantage. As a result of inflation, the value of money decreases over time, which means that a given amount of money will be able to purchase a smaller quantity of products and services.

Despite the fact that the overall price level is increasing, the value of assets that are resistant to inflation remains the same.

In addition, cryptocurrencies like as Bitcoin have a capped supply, which indicates that there is a maximum number of coins that can ever exist because of the restricted supply.

This scarcity can serve as a hedge against inflation because the value of the currency is not diluted by an ever-increasing supply. This is in contrast to standard fiat currencies, which allow governments to print additional money, which can lead to inflation of the currency.

Cost-effective transactions

The term "cost-effective transactions" refers to the financial efficiency that can be obtained by lowering or limiting the costs that are associated with activities such as making payments or moving money. This is because traditional banking systems frequently involve a number of intermediaries, each of whom adds their own fees, which ultimately results in the transaction being more expensive.

A further advantage of cryptocurrencies is that they provide a decentralized platform, which eliminates the requirement for a large number of intermediaries. Transaction costs can be greatly reduced as a result of this, making them more affordable for both individuals and corporations.

These kinds of cost-effective transactions are especially advantageous for overseas transfers, which are typically subject to excessive fees charged by traditional financial institutions. Through the simplification of procedures and the reduction of expenditures that are not essential, cryptocurrencies improve the accessibility and efficiency of financial transactions.

A decentralized system

The concept of decentralization is fundamental to many different types of systems, but it is especially important in the context of cryptocurrencies. What this indicates is that there is no single institution, such as a government or a central bank that has control over the entire network. Control, on the other hand, is decentralized among a number of different participants or nodes.

The verification of each transaction in a decentralized system is now carried out by a network of nodes rather than by a central authority. By doing so, we ensure that there is no single point of failure, which in turn improves the system's security and resilience.

However, despite the fact that decentralization increases accessibility and openness and frequently lowers costs, it also brings with it a number of issues, such as the possibility of difficulties in coordination and the complexity of regulatory requirements.

Accessibility

The term "accessibility" refers to the ease with which individuals are able to gain access to and make use of a service, product, or information, independent of any obstacles that may be brought about by their physical, financial, or technical circumstances. Accessibility, when applied to the realm of technology and online platforms, frequently entails the development of user interfaces that are accessible to all individuals, including those diagnosed with disabilities.

When it comes to cryptocurrencies, accessibility refers to the fact that everyone who possesses a digital wallet and an internet connection is able to take part in transactions. This eliminates the requirement for a traditional banking relationship.

Even more importantly, technology has the potential to empower those living in underserved or rural locations by providing them with the opportunity to participate in the global economy in ways that were previously inconceivable. It is through accessibility that inclusivity and equal opportunity are fostered.

Protection and safety

When we talk about safety and security, we are referring to the protection of information, assets, or systems against potential dangers and unauthorized access on their part. It contains comprehensive safeguards to guard against hacking, fraud, or misuse in the context of technology and money, including cryptocurrencies. These precautions are not limited to cryptocurrencies.

Furthermore, many cryptocurrencies offer great degrees of security since they make use of sophisticated encryption algorithms. The technology that underpins block-chain ensures that once a transaction is recorded, it cannot be altered, so giving a record that is both permanent and unchangeable.

Safety and security, on the other hand, are frequently dependent on the actions of users, such as maintaining the confidentiality of private keys. Although technology have the potential to offer comprehensive security, it is essential for users to be conscious of their actions and to engage in responsible behaviors in order to keep the environment safe and secure.

Transparency

To be transparent is to be clear, open, and honest in all sorts of communication, deals, or operations. Transparency is a quality that may be applied to any situation.

In the context of business or finance, transparency refers to the provision of information that is comprehensive, accurate, and up to date to all stakeholders, so enabling them to make decisions based on accurate information.

The adoption of block-chain technology, in which all transactions are recorded on a public ledger, has made it possible for the world of cryptocurrency to become more transparent through the implementation of this technology. Anyone is able to access this ledger, which guarantees that all operations are openly logged and can be independently verified.

Most importantly, transparency helps to generate trust since it ensures that parties are held accountable and assists in the prevention of unethical or fraudulent behavior, which in turn serves to foster confidence in the establishment or organization.

Confidentiality

The term "Confidentiality" refers to the rights that individuals have that enable them to maintain the confidentiality of their personal information and activities, as well as to protect them from having their data accessed or disclosed by unauthorized parties. Privacy is becoming an increasingly important issue in this day and age, particularly with regard to financial transactions.

To add insult to injury, when it comes to cryptocurrencies, privacy is a sword with two very different edges. In one sense, transactions are recorded on a public ledger, which guarantees that they are open to public scrutiny. On the other hand, the identities of the individuals engaged are frequently concealed and are only represented by cryptographic addresses.

Particularly crucial is the fact that this guarantees a certain level of anonymity, which enables users to carry out transactions without disclosing any personal information. Many people place a high value on the privacy that cryptocurrencies provide, yet this raises concerns about the possibility that they could be used for illegal activity.

Easy currency exchange

This is the straightforward and uncomplicated process of converting one currency into another. During the old banking system, the process of exchanging currency may require complicated procedures, fees, and occasionally delays.

The process can also be significantly simplified by using bitcoins, which is another advantage.

Users have the ability to easily exchange a variety of cryptocurrencies or convert them into fiat currency in real time through the use of a number of different platforms and digital wallets. This can be accomplished with just a few clicks from any location in the world, and a lot of the time at currency rates that are competitive.

In addition, the convenience and effectiveness of cryptocurrency trading make it an appealing choice for those who are traveling, conducting business on a global scale, or anybody else who has to manage numerous currencies with a minimum of friction.

Disadvantages of Cryptocurrency

Among the drawbacks of cryptocurrency is the substantial price fluctuation that it exhibits, which makes investments subject to danger.

A lack of regulation might raise the possibility of fraudulent activity or misuse.

Some users may be dissuaded from using the technology due to its complexity, and the amount of energy that is required to mine certain cryptocurrencies raises concerns about the environment. These elements are among the contributors to the more cautious approach that some investors and authorities take.

The following is a detailed explanation of the drawbacks associated with cryptocurrency, which are as follows:

Pseudonymous transactions

A way of conducting business in which parties are recognized by pseudonyms rather than by providing personal information is referred to as a pseudonymous transaction.

In the case of cryptocurrencies, users conduct transactions using anonymous alphanumeric addresses that are not directly connected to their identities in the real world.

While this does offer some degree of privacy and anonymity, it is important to note that nevertheless all transactions are still recorded on the public blockchain.

Although transactions conducted under pseudonyms provide advantages in terms of privacy, there is a possibility that they could be related with issues surrounding the possible misuse of illegal activity.

Constant risk of an attack

Inside the context of cryptocurrencies, the term "constant risk of an attack" refers to the ever-present danger that is posed by hackers and other malevolent entities who are attempting to take advantage of flaws that exist inside a system. Even with some of the most advanced cyber security techniques, there is no system that is completely safe.

In addition, cyberattacks can result in the theft of assets, the loss of personal information, or even the compromising of a network. The potential for an attack is always a concern, despite the fact that it is vital to maintain vigilance, perform frequent upgrades, and adhere to best practices in order to eliminate these risks completely.

Excessive power consumption

As stated previously, cryptocurrency mining methods, most notably Bitcoin mining, need a large amount of energy, which is referred to as excessive power consumption in the cryptocurrency industry. Mining requires a substantial amount of processing power because it involves extremely complicated calculations.

Now, there are situations in which the amount of energy utilized can be comparable to that of entire nations. Concerns about the environment have been expressed as a result of this, particularly if the energy originates from sources that are not renewable. Despite the fact that efforts are being made within the industry to limit this consumption, it continues to be a serious problem and a primary argument against the mainstream adoption of certain cryptocurrencies.

Lack of key policies

The absence of important rules in cryptocurrency refers to the absence of standardized regulations and guidelines that govern the use of digital currencies and the trading of those currencies. Investors, users, and authorities all face issues as a result of this regulatory vacuum, which can lead to confusion and inconsistency.

Additionally, the lack of clear standards may result in unethical practices, fraudulent activities, or the inappropriate usage of cryptocurrencies. This highlights the importance of having regulations that are consistent, which not only offer security but also encourage innovation within the realm of digital currencies, which is constantly going through rapid change.

Costly network participation

The term "costly network participation" in the context of cryptocurrency refers to the substantial financial commitment that is necessary to become a miner or to run a complete node operation within specific block-chain networks. Particularly in highly competitive mining markets such as Bitcoin, the hardware, electricity, and continuous maintenance can be quite pricey.

It is more crucial to note that these high costs have the potential to discourage individual participation and result in the concentration of mining power in the hands of a small number of huge entities. One element of certain cryptocurrency systems that poses a challenge to the goal of decentralized control and inclusion is the presence of this aspect.

CHAPTER FIVE

Getting Started with Crypto Trading

Before you can begin using cryptocurrency, you will need to create a cryptocurrency wallet that is capable of storing both the public and private keys that are required to verify that the coins you possess correctly belong to you. For individuals who are new to the world of cryptocurrency, this may appear to be a frightening concept; yet, it is only a few steps away.

The process can be broken down into four primary parts.

- ❖ Selecting the sort of wallet that is most suitable for your needs.
- ❖ Create a user account.
- ❖ Purchase the necessary hardware, or download the software that is required.

❖ Configure your security features, including a recovery phrase, and be sure to do so.

To acquire cryptocurrency, you can either transfer coins from another wallet or exchange or purchase cryptocurrency.

Different kinds of cryptocurrency wallets

Three primary categories of wallets to choose from.

One choice is a software wallet, often known as a hot wallet, which stores your cryptocurrency on a device that you own and that is linked to the internet.

Another choice that offers an additional layer of protection is a cold wallet, which is a specialized piece of hardware that stores your cryptocurrency in an offline environment.

Custodial wallets are yet another option for storing cryptocurrency. These wallets allow you to leave your cryptocurrency in the custody of a reputable organization, such as a cryptocurrency exchange.

How to create a wallet for cryptocurrency

Software wallet

Creating a software wallet:

- ❖ To begin, select a wallet application and download it on either a desktop computer or a mobile device; the majority of software wallets offer both options.

- ❖ Create an account for yourself. Due to the fact that you will not be required to manually enter any personal information, this procedure will be rather simple in comparison to other techniques.

- Instead, you will be required to devise a security technique, such as applying a password or utilizing facial recognition technology.

- Write down your "seed" or recovery phrase. The application will generate a random phrase consisting of twelve or twenty-four words that corresponds to your private key when you create your account. In the event that you misplace your login credentials or wish to retrieve them on a different device, you will not be able to access your funds without it, thus it is imperative that you preserve this phrase in a secure location.

❖ Put some cryptocurrency in your wallet. You are able to accomplish this by transferring tokens from a different wallet or by attaching your account to an exchange inside the settings of the app, both of which will require further verification.

Hardware wallets

In contrast to non-custodial wallets, hardware wallets keep your keys on a physical device that may be connected to your computer or phone via a USB connector, WiFi, or QR code. Hardware wallets are not considered to be custodial wallets. They are more difficult to operate and are more secure than other options since they keep your data completely offline.

A hardware wallet can be set up in the following manner:

Purchase the device

It is possible to purchase hardware wallets directly from the firms who manufacture them; additionally, some of them are sold in retail establishments such as Best Buy and Walmart.

Upon its arrival, you will be required to turn it on, and you could be asked to generate a personal identification number (PIN).

Download the software

The software that is compatible with the hardware wallet brands is something that you will need to install in order to set up your device and transfer funds.

Additionally, some desktop applications come equipped with built-in capabilities that allow you to connect your wallet to platforms that provide decentralized finance applications or exchanges. Remember to write down your 12- or 24-word seed phrase and store it in a secure location when you establish an account. Use this phrase to identify yourself.

Connect your device

It is possible to connect your hardware wallet to internet software in a few different methods, which will allow you to transfer tokens and make transactions. A USB cord is required to connect certain devices to your computer, while others can connect wirelessly through the use of a QR code or WiFi. There ought to be instructions included with your device that explain how to configure this.

Add cryptocurrency to your wallet

A number of cold wallets are equipped with features that enable users to purchase cryptocurrency and then load it onto their smartphone for offline safekeeping. Furthermore, you are able to migrate tokens from an exchange or another wallet that you already have by using the address of your wallet.

Custodial wallet

Trusted third-party providers are in charge of managing custodial wallets, which are also referred to as hosted wallets. They make it possible for users to keep assets directly on the exchange, which facilitates easy access to trade.

In the event that you lose your login credentials, custodial wallets also come equipped with a built-in password recovery feature. This makes them an excellent choice for users who are just starting out or who are seeking for a more hands-off approach.

Setting up a custodial crypto wallet:

Find a trustworthy platform

This is especially crucial for custodial wallets because you do not have control over your private keys. In addition to being simple to use, the top exchanges for holding cryptocurrency safeguard your money against any potential security breaches. In addition to that, they offer some form of protection against financial loss.

Sign up for an account.

After you have decided which platform you will use, locate the registration page on either a desktop computer or a mobile device.

Afterwards, you will need to establish an account by providing your email address and coming up with a password.

Depending on the circumstances, you could be required to provide personal information such as your date of birth, date of birth, Social Security number, and legal name. In addition, for verification purposes, you could be required to input a code that was sent to your phone number and upload a picture of your photo identification.

Add cryptocurrency to your wallet

Once you have logged in, you will be able to use the address of your new wallet to move cryptocurrency from another wallet. This is because your account on the exchange functions as a wallet. By linking your bank account to the exchange, you can also make direct purchases of coins by using the exchange.

You are able to use debit or credit cards, as well as wire transfers or ACH, to make payments with the majority of exchanges. The fees may change depending on the mode of payment.

A Guide to Purchasing Cryptocurrency

In order to ensure the safety of its transactions and to exercise control over the production of new units, cryptocurrencies are digital or virtual tokens that make use of encryption. Bitcoin and other cryptocurrencies are frequently purchased with "fiat" or traditional currencies such as the United States dollar or the euro.

On the other hand, another option is to purchase them using cryptocurrencies such as Bitcoin or Ethereum. When you want to acquire cryptocurrencies, the first thing you need to do is create a digital wallet to keep your money.

Following that, you will be able to purchase coins on a cryptocurrency exchange by using either your standard currency or another cryptocurrency.

Stages involved in purchasing cryptocurrency.

Step 1: **Choosing a platform**

Determining which platform to employ is the first stage in the process. You have the option of selecting either a conventional broker or a cryptocurrency exchange that is specialized to your needs:

Typical brokers and dealers

These are online brokers that provide a variety of options for buying and selling cryptocurrencies, in addition to traditional financial assets such as equities, bonds, and exchange-traded funds (ETFs). With these platforms, trading prices are typically lower, but there are fewer crypto features available.

Cryptocurrency exchanges

A wide variety of cryptocurrency exchanges are available for users to select from, each of which provides a unique selection of cryptocurrencies, wallet storage, interest-bearing account options, and many features. Asset-based fees are charged by a number of exchanges.

When doing a comparison between various platforms, it is important to take into consideration the cryptocurrencies that are available, the fees that are charged, the security features, the storage and withdrawal choices, and any educational resources that are available.

Step 2: Funding your account

When you have decided on a platform, the next step is to ensure that your account is adequately funded so that you may start trading. Despite the fact that this varies from platform to platform, the majority of cryptocurrency exchanges enable users to purchase cryptocurrency using fiat currencies, which are currencies that are issued by governments, such as the United States Dollar, the British Pound, or the Euro, using their debit or credit cards.

It is deemed hazardous to make cryptocurrency purchases using credit cards, which is why certain exchanges do not offer this method. Additionally, there are credit card providers who do not permit cryptocurrency transactions.

This is due to the fact that cryptocurrencies are extremely volatile, and it is not a good idea to take the risk of going into debt for certain assets, as this could result in paying high credit card transaction fees.

On some platforms, ACH transfers and wire transfers are also acceptable forms of payment. Each platform has its own set of accepted payment methods, as well as its own set of processing times for deposits and withdrawals. In a similar vein, the amount of time it takes for deposits to become available varies depending on the method of payment.

Fees are an essential aspect to take into consideration. These fees include potential fees for transactions involving deposits and withdrawals, as well as fees for trading. It is important to do some preliminary research on the fees, as they will differ depending on the platform and the method of payment.

Step 3: Placing an order

You have the option of placing an order through the mobile platform or web interface of your broker or exchange. If you are interested in purchasing cryptocurrencies, you can do so by clicking "buy," selecting the type of order you want to place, entering the quantity of cryptocurrencies you wish to buy, and then confirming the order. When it comes to "sell" orders, the same procedure applies.

Alternative methods of investing in cryptocurrency

It is possible for consumers to buy, sell, or keep cryptocurrencies through the use of payment systems such as PayPal, Cash App, & Venmo. It is also important to note that the following investment instruments are available:

Bitcoin trusts: You can buy shares of Bitcoin trusts with a conventional brokerage account. These vehicles provide ordinary investors exposure to bitcoin through the stock market.

Bitcoin mutual funds: There are Bitcoin ETFs and Bitcoin mutual funds to pick from.

Blockchain stocks or ETFs: You can indirectly invest in cryptocurrency by purchasing shares of blockchain firms that specialise in the technology powering cryptocurrency and crypto transactions.

CHAPTER SIX

Introduction to Technical Analysis

The technical analysis of cryptocurrencies is the first step towards determining current crypto market volatility and identifying market movements and breakouts.

This includes comprehending cryptocurrency charts, digital currency statistics, and market patterns. To put it simply, investors want to buy when the market is at its lowest and sell when it reaches its peak. Trading cryptocurrency, like regular trading, requires precise timing.

A detailed crypto technical analysis is one way to determine whether you're investing at the proper time. "Is the coin still too high?" When analyzing data, you should ask yourself questions such as "will it drop lower?"

Fundamentally, technical analysis assumes that markets follow trends that will eventually replicate themselves. Its goal is to detect these continuous variations and predict future market patterns, allowing the trader to purchase and sell at the optimal time.

Key Components of Crypto Technical Analysis.

When conducting cryptocurrency technical analysis, there are several crucial components to consider. Each is critical to effectively understanding, predicting, and strategizing your upcoming cryptocurrency trades. Let's take a closer look at the key parts of the cryptocurrency technical analysis puzzle.

Price action

Price action is fundamental to cryptocurrency technical analysis. This shows the movement of a cryptocurrency's price over time, as depicted on a chart. By observing price movements, you can start to uncover trends and patterns that will help guide your future investments.

Cryptocurrency charts

Cryptocurrency charts show how prices have changed over time. Different types of charts, including as line charts, bar charts, and candlestick charts, provide distinct viewpoints on price movement and are essential tools in a crypto analyst's toolbox.

Volume

Another important factor is volume, which measures the total quantity of coins moved in a certain period. Volume reveals the strength or weakness of a price movement and can predict probable market turning moments.

Market trends

Identifying and analyzing market patterns is critical in crypto technical analysis. Trends, whether upward, downward, or sideways, can provide valuable insights into anticipated future price changes.

Technical Indicators

Finally, technical indicators are mathematical calculations that use a cryptocurrency's price and volume. Various indicators, such as moving averages or the relative strength index, can help predict future price changes and provide buy or sell recommendations.

As you can see, cryptocurrency technical analysis is a multifaceted procedure. Understanding and utilizing these essential components will allow you to make more educated judgements in the often unpredictable realm of bitcoin trading.

Chart Patterns and Trend Analysis for Cryptocurrency

After learning the principles of crypto technical analysis, it's time to focus on one of the most important areas of cryptocurrency trading: chart patterns and trend analysis. Recognizing chart patterns and analyzing trends are critical for effectively forecasting the future movements of a cryptocurrency's price.

Cryptocurrency Chart Patterns

Chart patterns in the market can sometimes indicate the possibility of continuous or approaching price movement, signaling a trading opportunity. Keep a watch out for the following essential patterns:

Head and Shoulders: This pattern signals a reversal trend, implying that the bitcoin price may soon shift direction.

Double Top: This is a bearish reversal pattern that suggests potential downward pressure on the price.

Triangle patterns: Depending on their type (ascending, descending, or symmetrical), can indicate either bullish or bearish price action.

Trend Analysis

Meanwhile, trend analysis is the process of examining the movement of bitcoin prices to determine a direction (upward, downward, or sideways). There are some tendencies that traders should be aware of:

Bullish: An upward tendency that indicates higher prices.

Bearish: A downward trend with declining prices.

Consolidation: Consolidating occurs when the price looks to be moving laterally, signaling a pause in the trend.

Understanding and recognizing these chart patterns and trends may allow you to anticipate the next move in the cryptocurrency market before others do. However, while they might provide useful insights, they should not be depended on alone; always back up your findings with other areas of your technical analysis.

Importance of Volume and Volatility in Crypto Technical Analysis

Volume and volatility are critical components of cryptocurrency technical analysis. They frequently provide important signals to the underlying variations in market sentiment and can be utilized to forecast prospective price fluctuations. But what precisely do volume and volatility mean in the bitcoin context?

Understanding volume in cryptocurrency.

In layman's terms, volume refers to the total quantity of coins traded over a given time period. It is a measure of market activity and interest in a specific coin. Higher volume frequently indicates more liquidity and stability, which gives speculative traders with much-needed confidence in both buying and selling opportunities.

A quick increase in volume may signify a significant shift in market sentiment. For example, if there is a significant increase in trade volume in conjunction with a price increase, it frequently indicates a positive trend. In contrast, if the trade volume drops dramatically while the price falls, it may indicate a bearish trend. Thus, recognizing volume is an important part of projecting market behavior.

Volatility in Cryptocurrency Technical Analysis

Volatility is defined as the pace at which the price of a cryptocurrency rises or falls in response to a certain set of returns. Cryptocurrencies, by their very nature, are more volatile than traditional fiat currencies. This means that the price of a cryptocurrency might fluctuate dramatically in a short period of time, allowing investors to profit or lose significantly.

An increase in volatility results in a more vibrant and dynamic trading environment with higher risk and reward. However, due to its volatility, cryptocurrency investing frequently creates a scenario similar to the Wild West, in which fortune and risk are closely linked. Thus, understanding and tracking volatility becomes critical in technical analysis.

Technical Indicators and Their Importance in Crypto-analysis

In the field of cryptocurrency technical analysis, technical indicators are critical. These are statistical techniques that help traders examine and interpret market movements, allowing them to make more informed trading decisions. Crypto analysts use technical indicators to measure market momentum and trends, with the ultimate goal of forecasting future price moves.

Understanding the various types of technical indicators

Technical indicators are typically classified into four types: trend, momentum, volatility, and volume indicators. Each has its own distinct function within the context of technical analysis.

Trend Indicators

As the name implies, trend indicators (or trend-following indicators) are designed to detect the presence and direction of a trend. This can help traders choose the optimal timing to engage or exit a trade. The Moving Average (MA) is a common trend indicator.

Momentum indicators

Momentum indicators help traders detect the rate at which the price of a cryptocurrency is changing. These indicators, which assess the strength of a trend, might provide insights about probable reversals or rallies. When it comes to momentum indicators, the Relative Strength Index (RSI) is a popular choice.

Volatility Indicators

Because volatility is a key feature of the cryptocurrency market, volatility indicators are particularly valuable in crypto technical analysis. They aid in determining the rate at which an asset's price rises or falls in response to a given set of returns. Bollinger Bands is a widely used volatility indicator.

Volume indicators

These tools allow traders to see how many crypto currencies were traded over a given time period. On-Balance Volume (OBV) and Volume Rate of Change (ROC) are common volume metrics.

Common Pitfalls in Crypto Technical Analysis

It's indisputable that crypto technical analysis is a useful instrument for entering the cryptocurrency market. However, as with any tool, its value is dependent on the user's understanding and application. To use it properly, one must understand the common pitfalls.

Overconfidence with Technical Analysis Tools

An overreliance on chart patterns and indicators might be a serious mistake. It is critical to recognize that technical analysis is not a crystal ball that can forecast future market activity with full certainty. While it gives useful information, it is still reliant on past price movements, which are not always reliable predictors of future performance.

Disregard Market News and Events

It's easy to become so focused on charts and patterns that you lose sight of other important factors driving the market. News events, government actions, technology advancements, and market attitudes all play a role in cryptocurrency trading, and while these elements may not appear on a chart, they can radically alter the patterns and predictions made by technical analysts.

Incorrect use of technical indicators

Misinterpretation or inappropriate application of technical indications can easily result in disastrously poor conclusions. For example, depending on a single signal may result in a narrow and potentially inaccurate perspective of the market. It is crucial to use several indicators and look at the big picture.

Lack of a structured trading plan

One of the most common hazards for newcomers in technical analysis is entering the market without a set approach. Trading cryptocurrencies without a strategy is similar to swimming turbulent waters without a map; it raises the likelihood of making rash decisions and succumbing to market volatility. A trader's success depends on his or her ability to define clear entry and exit points, comprehend risk management, and set reasonable profit expectations.

To summarize, while technical analysis provides a methodical approach to trading, it must be utilized with caution, understanding its limitations, and in conjunction with strong decision-making and risk management strategies.

Thank you for purchasing this book, for more on crypto technical analysis get my book on crypto technical analysis.

Happy trading!!

Bonus package

Here's a link for accessing a forex video course.

subscribepage.io/freeforexcourse

www.ingramcontent.com/pod-product-compliance
Lightning Source LLC
Chambersburg PA
CBHW050303230526
45471CB00005B/2000